The Delightful
THAM
and Chilter

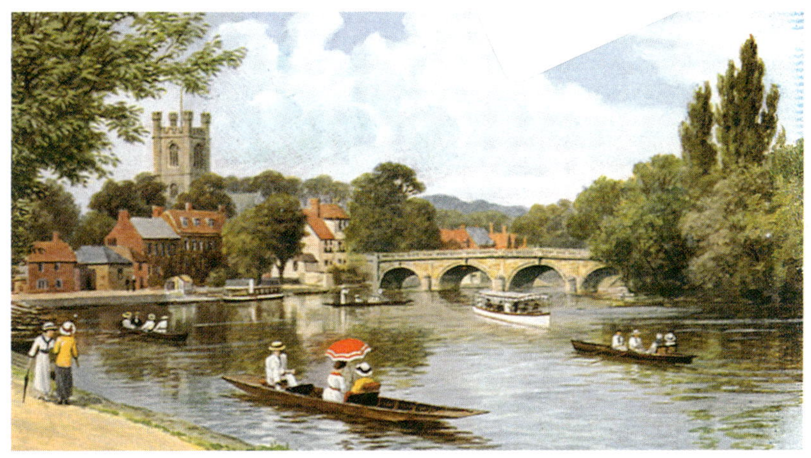

Sweet Thames! runne softly till I end my song

Edmund Spenser

Painted by A. R. Quinton
and H. Sutton Palmer R.I.
with drawings by Joseph Pennell
and Frederick L. Griggs

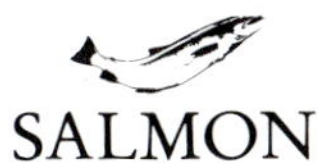

SALMON

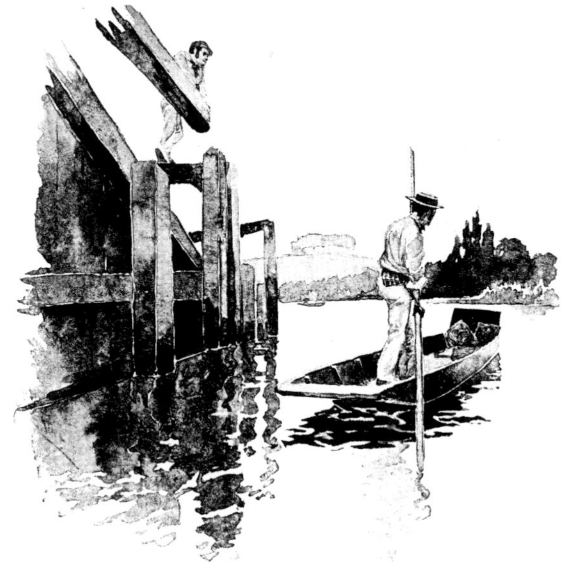

Published by J Salmon Limited,
100 London Road, Sevenoaks, Kent TN13 1BB

First edition 1995

Designed by the Salmon Studio

ISBN 1 898435 35 9

Printed in England by J Salmon Limited, Tubs Hill Works, Sevenoaks, Kent

Coloured Illustrations

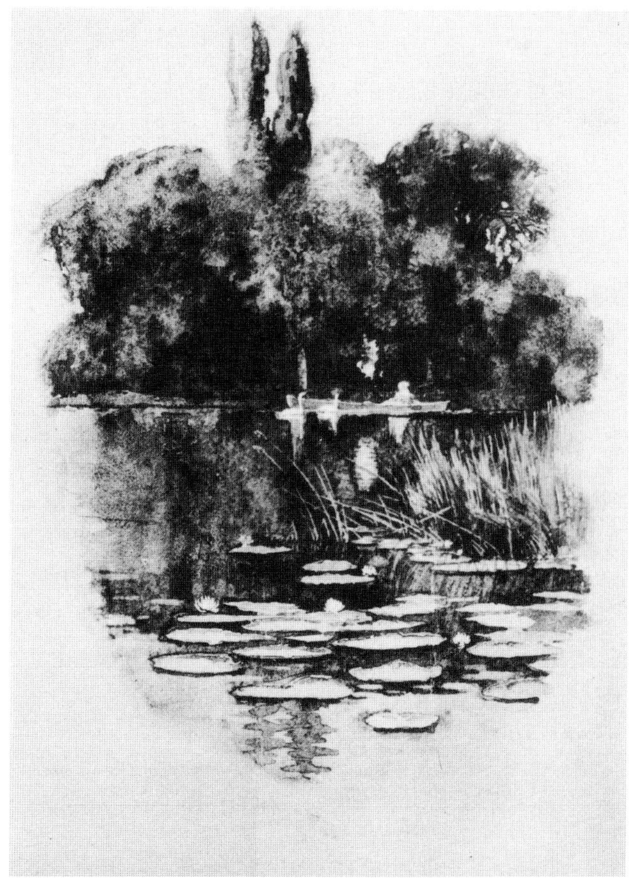

Slow let us trace the matchless vale of Thames
James Thomson

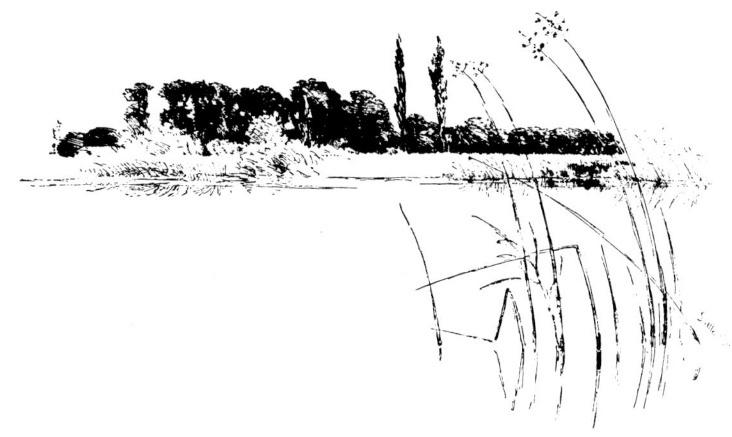

THAMES HEAD TO OXFORD

The source of the Churn, at Seven Springs, is claimed to be the farthest from the sea of all Thames water, but the true Thames Head is to be found in a flat meadow to the south-westward of Cirencester. Here from a pool barely 400 feet above sea-level the river begins its journey, winding among pastures. Through a country of wide open spaces it flows, receiving the waters of the Churn and Coln and Leach, to Lechlade, the first of the real Thames-towns.

The tall steeple of Lechlade church marks the head of navigation like a full-stop. Below the town is St. John's Lock, where an ancient toll crossing carries the Fairford to Faringdon road across the river – it dates from 1229 although the present bridge was built in 1820. The next lock on the river is Buscot, its attendant church notable for a fine Burne-Jones window.

Between Lechlade and Radcot is Kelmscott, whose name has been made widely known by its association with William Morris; he bought the manor house in 1871. His grave lies in the churchyard, and the manor house itself is grand in its fine proportions. Radcot Bridge, a few miles to the east, was the scene of a skirmish in the Civil War – hereabouts the scenery is dominated by Faringdon Clump, a knoll of some 500 feet rising out of the flat country. The next bridge is Newbridge, which, as is usual in such cases, proves to be one of the oldest on the river – its low, deep stone arches date from 1260.

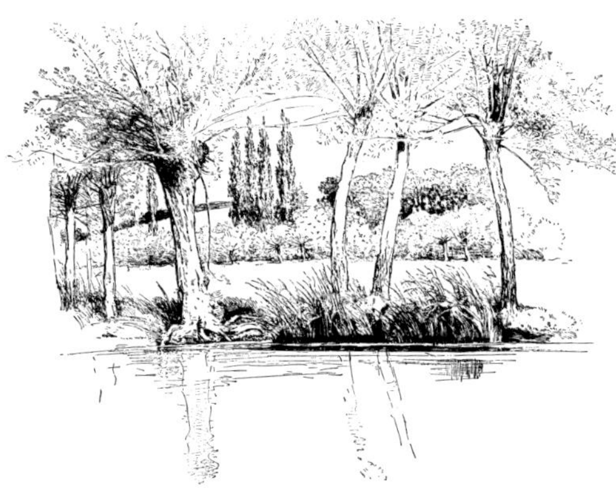

As Oxford nears, and passing Bablockhithe, Eynsham and Godstow with its ever popular Trout Inn beside the water, the river is still a country stream – yet only a few miles away across the Oxford loop, between Iffley and Sandford, it assumes a more majestic course. From Bablockhithe Ferry to Iffley in a straight line is only six miles, but by river it is fully twice that distance during which the Thames receives the flow of two major tributaries, the Evenlode and Cherwell. It is, however, Oxford, the city of dreaming spires, which marks the true boundary between the infant waters of the Upper Thames and the more majestic course of the river's middle reaches.

THE ROUND HOUSE, INGLESHAM

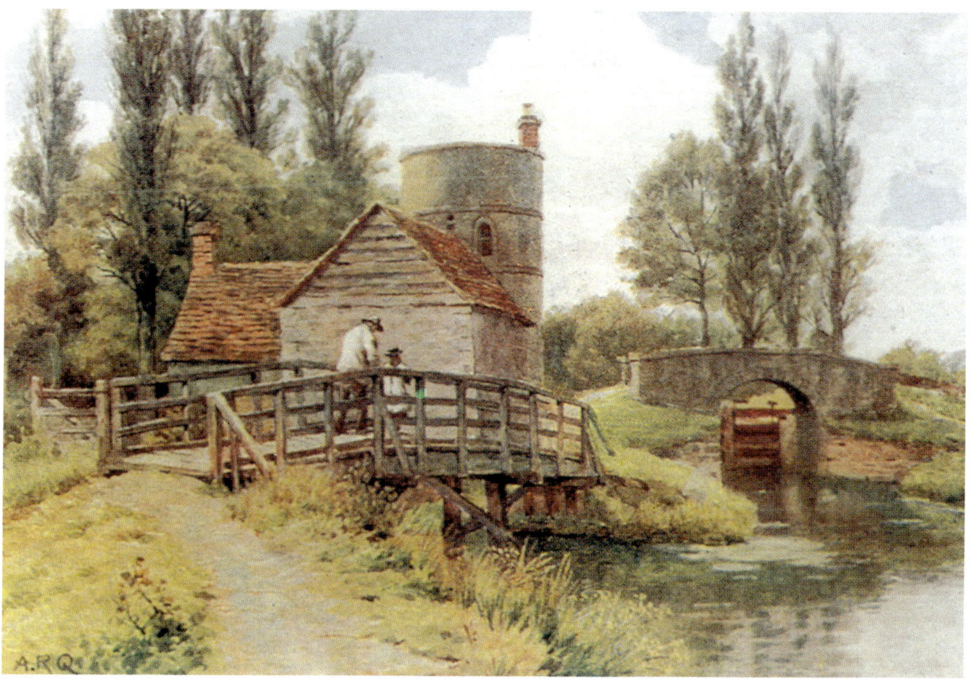

A river pleasant to behold,
  Embroidered all with fresh flowers gay,
Where, through the gravel, bright as any gold,
  The crystal water ran so clear and cold.

King James I

HAYMAKING AT LECHLADE

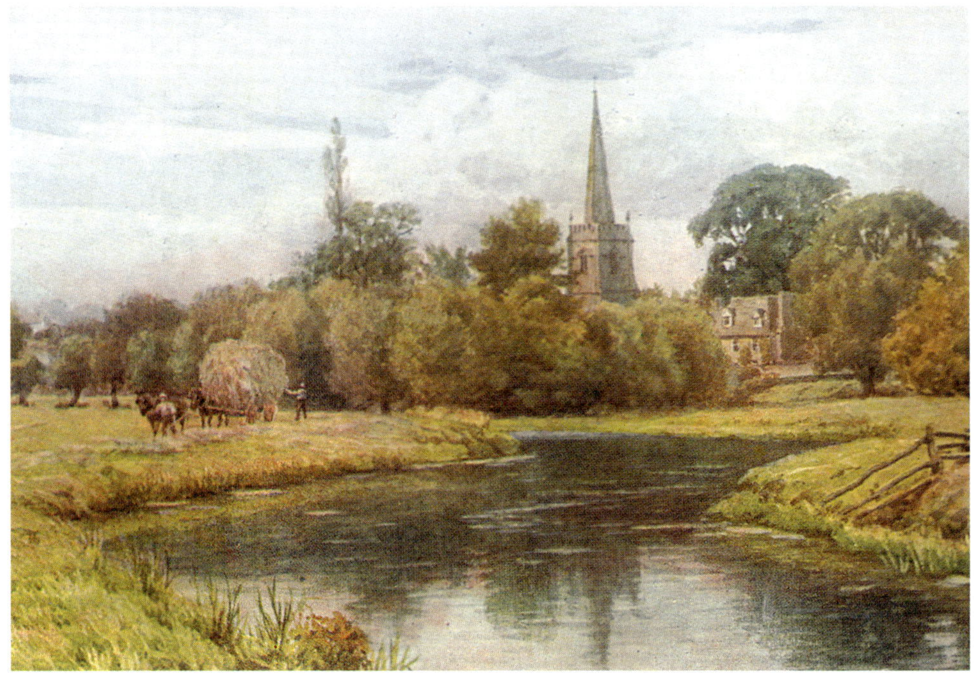

Like thee, noble river, like thee,
  Let our lives in beginning and ending,
Fair in their gathering be,
  And great in the time of their spending.
Isa Knox

NEWBRIDGE AND THE ROSE REVIVED INN

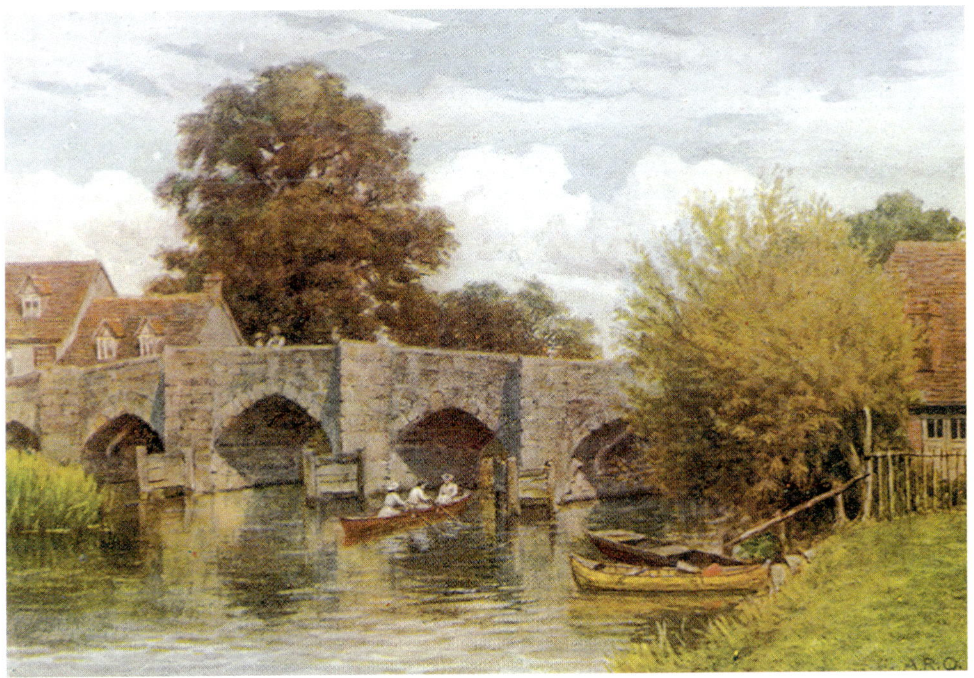

A lapping river-ripple all day chiding
  The bow of my wherry gliding
Down Thames, between his flowery shores
  Re-echoing to the oars.

Robert Bridges

THE WEIR STREAM AT PINKHILL

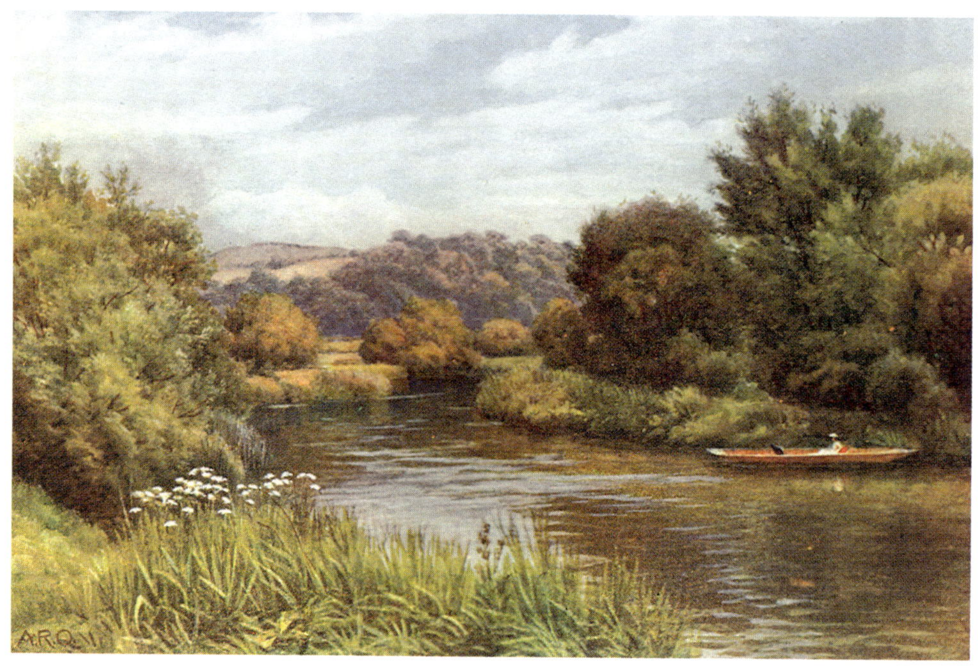

Ne'er saw I, never felt, a calm so deep!
The river glideth at his own sweet will.
William Wordsworth

THE BRIDGE AND TROUT INN, GODSTOW

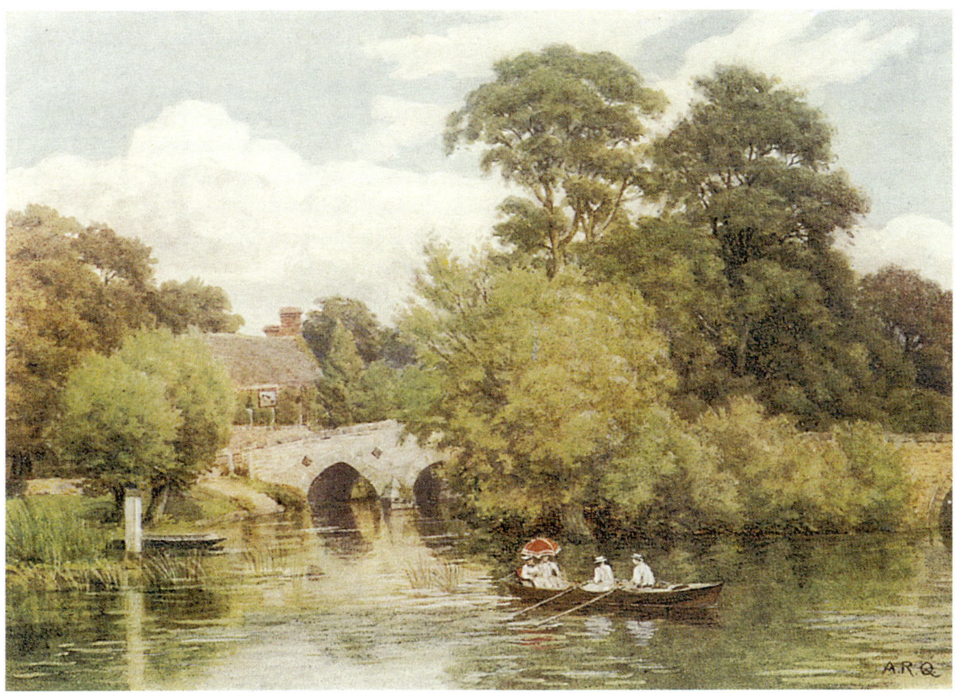

One knows of no single stream which presents such an endless variety of changing beauties as does the Thames.

Sydney Crossley

AT ABINGDON

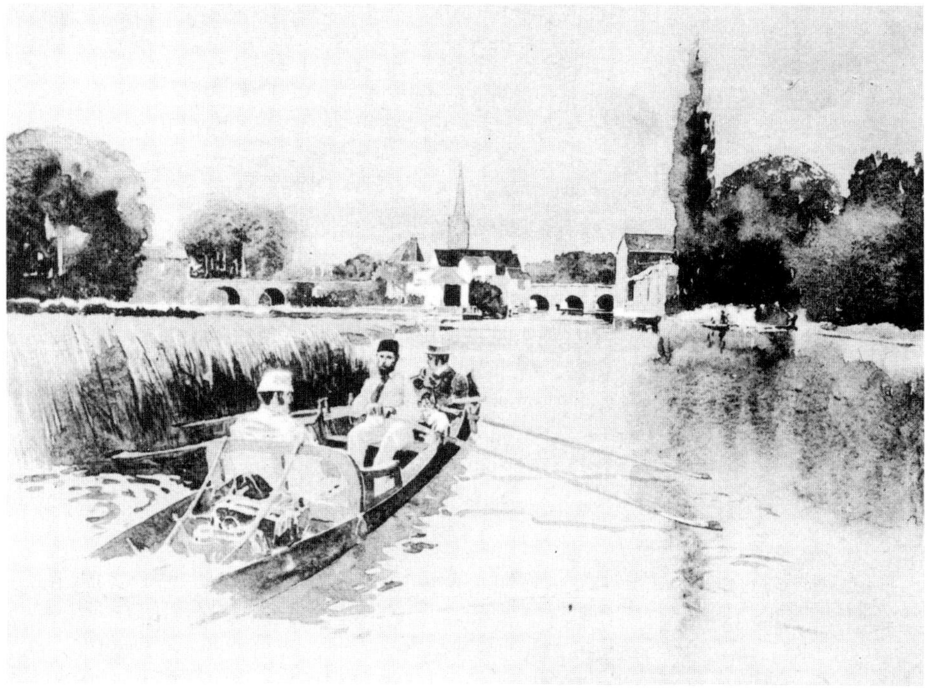

We rowed on between walls of tall reeds, whose population of reed sparrows and warblers was delightfully restless, twittering and chuckling as the wash of the boats stirred the reeds from the water in the still, hot morning.

William Morris

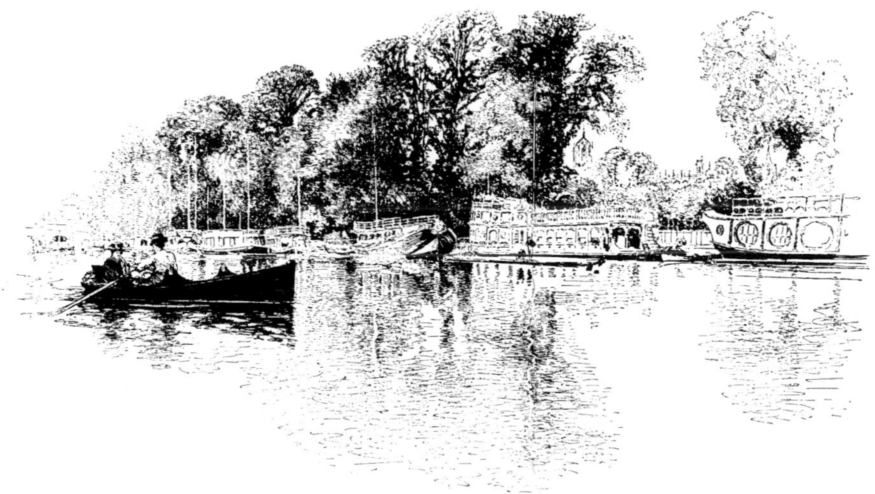

College barges at Oxford

OXFORD TO READING

Below Oxford the Thames has a brisk yet unhurried flow; here, a long straight reach from Shillingford Bridge looks down to Benson Church standing at the far bend backed by the Chiltern beech-woods; there, a series of twisting curves brings one suddenly close under the steep, sharp hills of Sinodun, with Wittenham Clumps poised gracefully on their summits. Here is the key point of the whole of this stretch of river. The hills command a sweep of country up the main valley towards Oxford and beyond, up the Vale of White Horse and up to the long dim line of Cotswold foothills.

The distinctive outline of Wittenham Clumps stands aloft of two of the most charming reaches of all the rural Thames – upstream from Shillingford to Day Lock and Abingdon and down past Benson to Wallingford. One can take the Abingdon road, passing the old cottages of Clifton Hampden, where the little church makes a fine picture high above the river. Perhaps take the lane that runs straight at Long Wittenham from Sinodun, past the village cross, or follow another by-road to the broad street of Sutton Courtenay. Close by is Dorchester with its fine abbey church; now little more than a large village but once a bishopric, one of the earliest in the Midlands. Finally ancient Abingdon and Wallingford are both places where it is a delight to wander around street after street and come across a charming town house,an old inn or an imposing market hall.

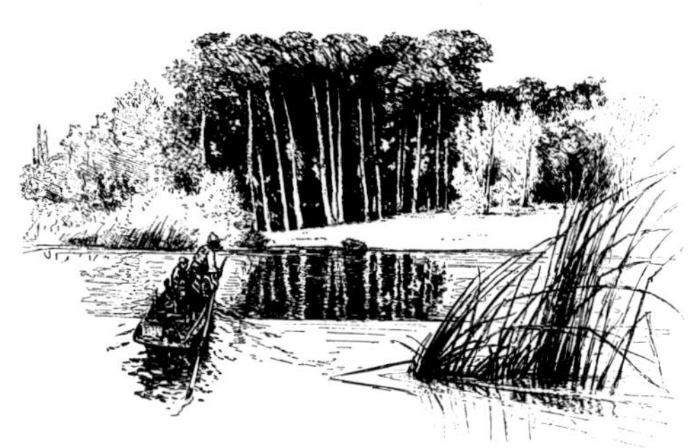

South of Wallingford the stretch to Reading is a mere ten miles, but through the Goring Gap the whole scene and atmosphere change. The hills stand high and close, with 500 feet heights only a couple of miles apart on either side of the river, where farms climb up as far as cultivation can struggle. Here the twin villages of Goring and Streatley, and Pangbourne and Whitchurch, hug the valley sides before the river approaches Reading, flowing through the open meadows around picturesquely situated Mapledurham Lock.

IFFLEY MILL

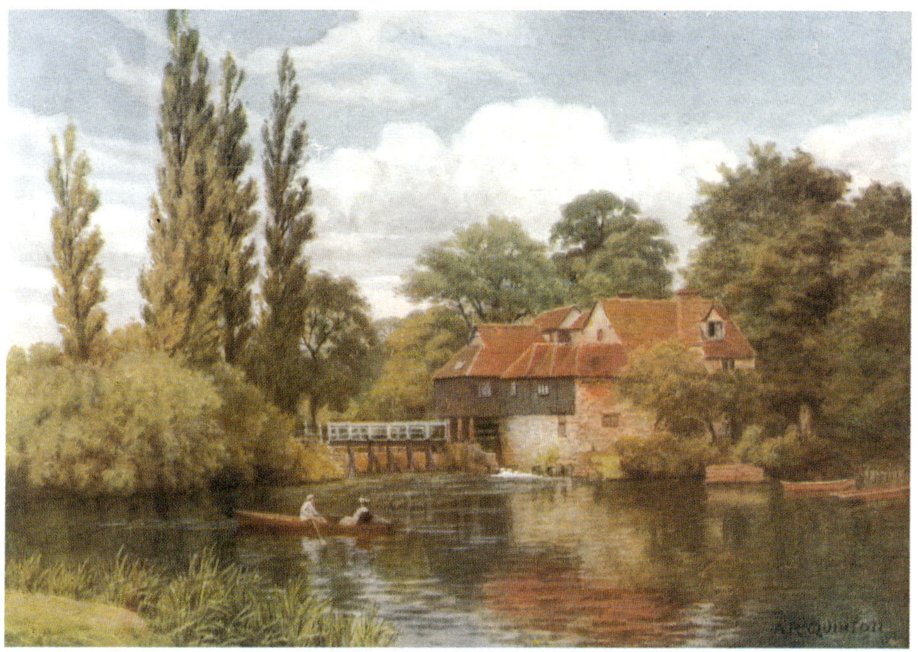

Though deep, yet clear; though gentle, yet not dull;
Strong without rage, without o'erflowing full.

Sir John Denham

NUNEHAM PARK

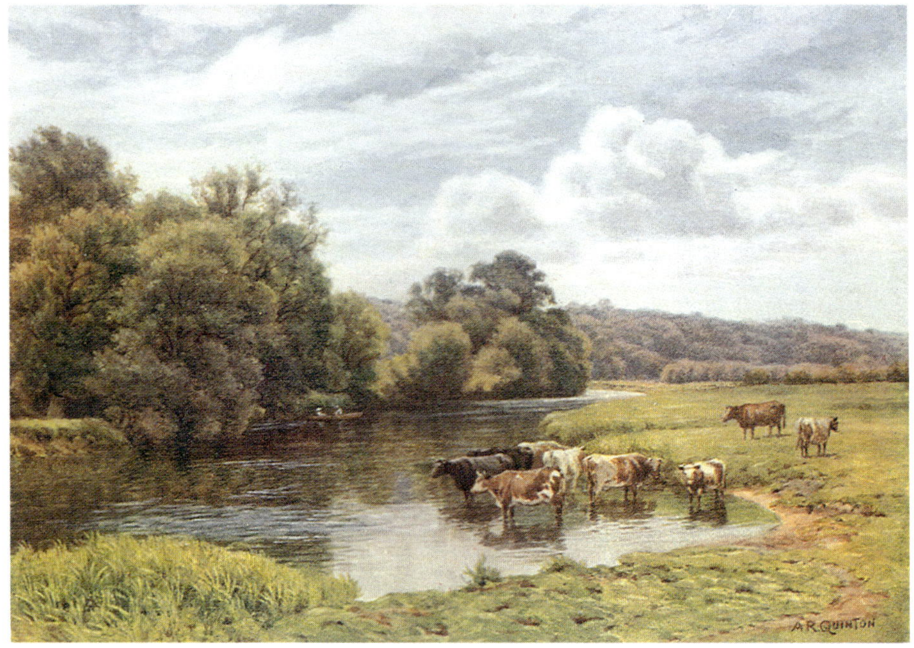

Along the shores of silver-streaming Themmes;
  Whose rutty bank, the which his river hemmes,
Was painted all with variable flowers

Edmund Spenser

AT CLIFTON HAMPDEN

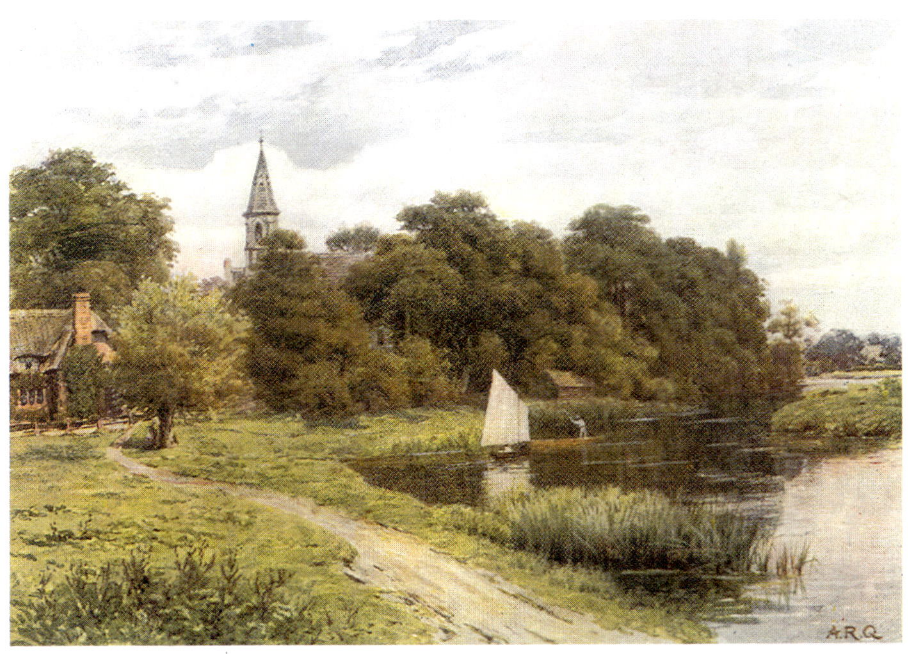

O glide, fair stream, for ever so
  Thy quiet soul on all bestowing,
Till all our minds for ever flow
  As thy deep waters now are flowing.

William Wordsworth

WALLINGFORD BRIDGE

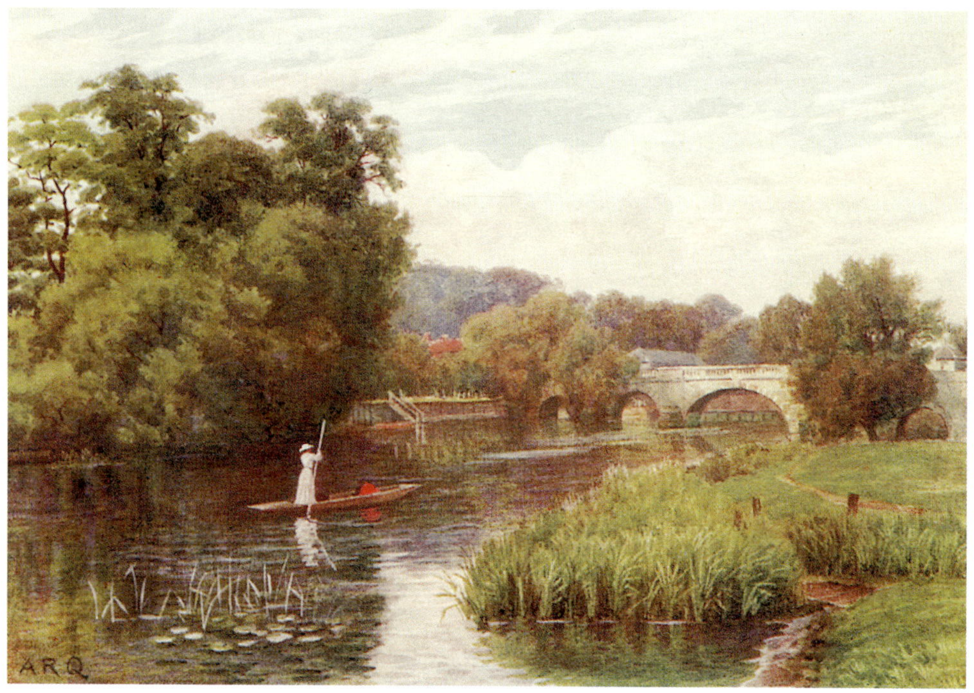

There grew broad flag-flowers,
  purple pranked with white,
And starry river-buds among the sedge,
  And floating water-lilies, broad and bright.

Percy Bysshe Shelley

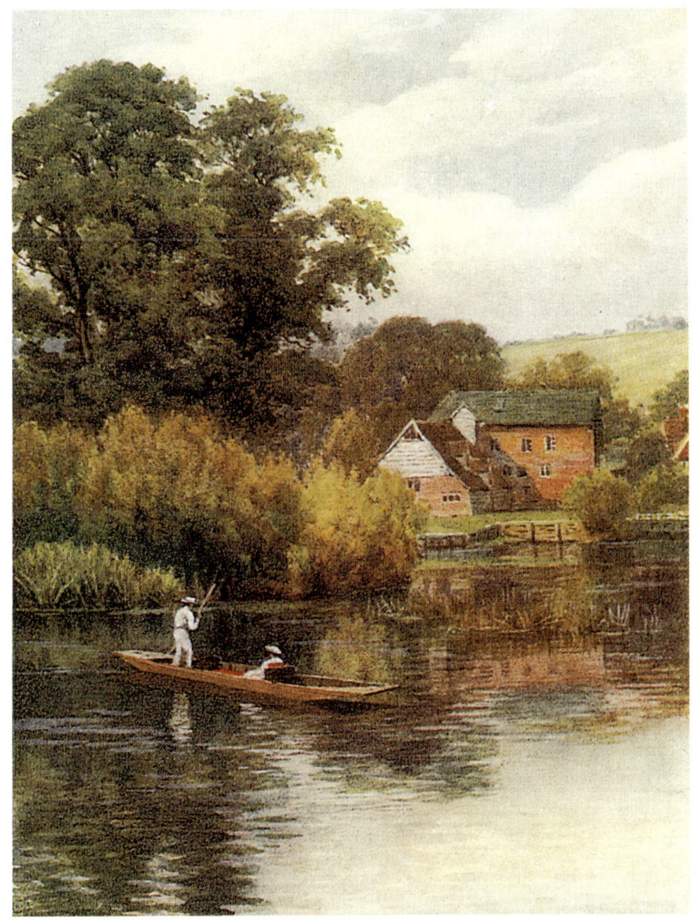

STREATLEY MILL

THE SWAN INN, PANGBOURNE

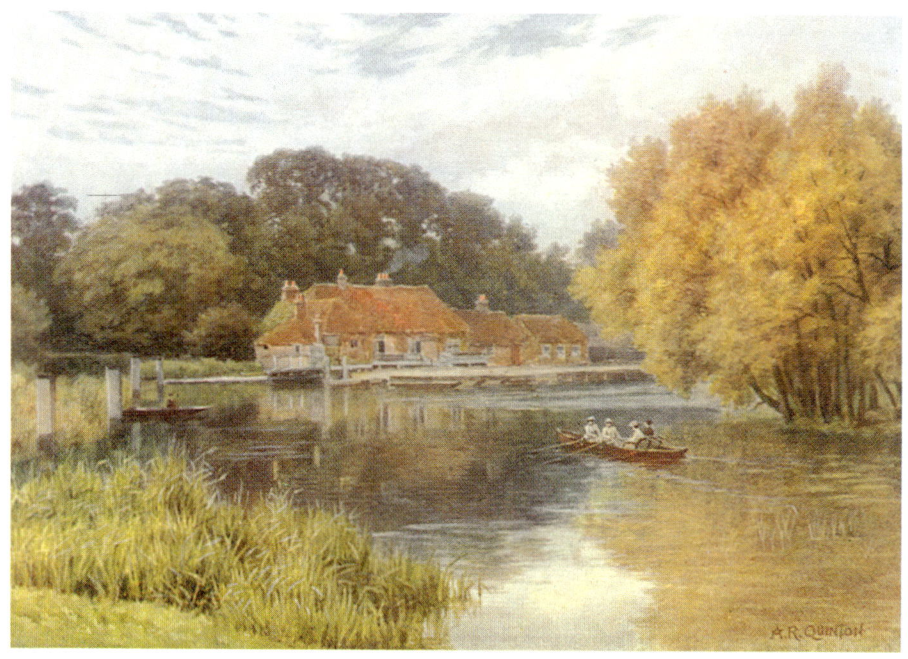

How calm! how still! the only sound
The dripping of our oar suspended.
William Wordsworth

MAPLEDURHAM LOCK

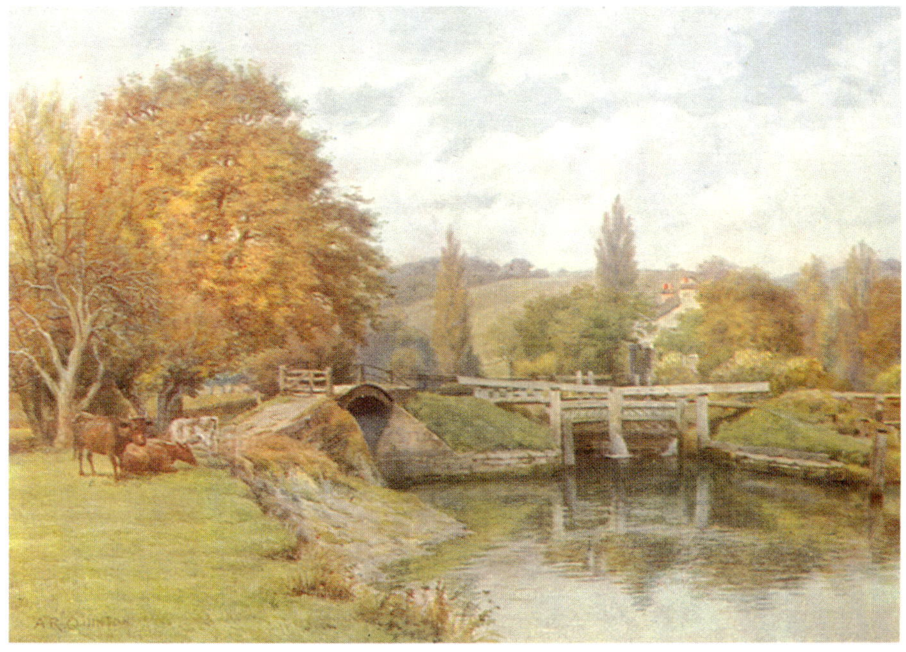

Grander scenery than that offered by Mapledurham, Cliveden, Marlow, Sonning, or the woods of Wytham is, of course, to be found in many places. But where is the simple rustic beauty of the Thames to be found elsewhere?

Sydney Crossley

AT HENLEY

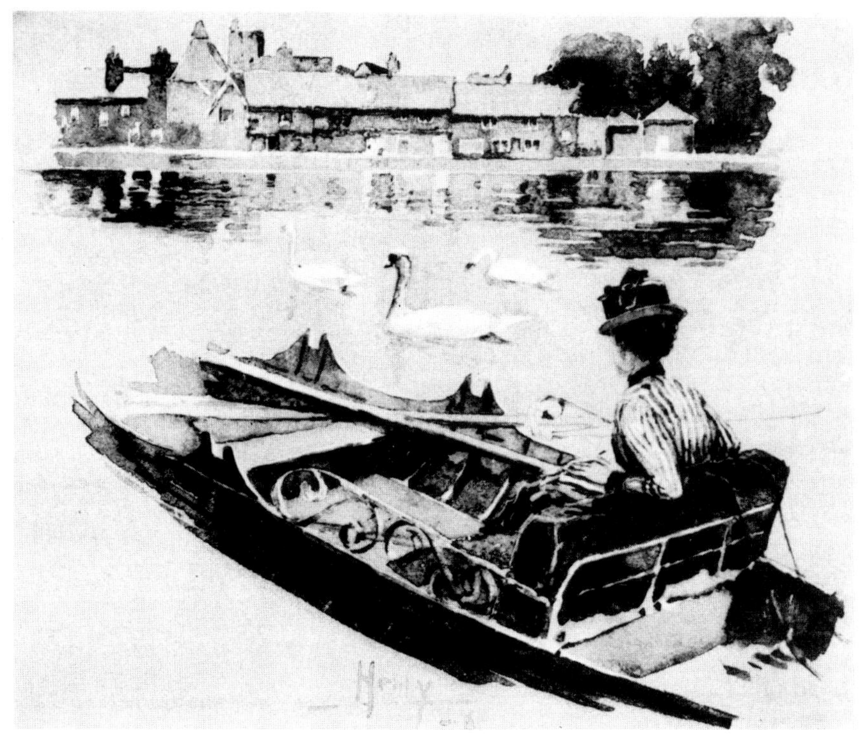

The swan with arched neck
  Between her white wings mantling,
Proudly rows her state with oary feet.

John Milton

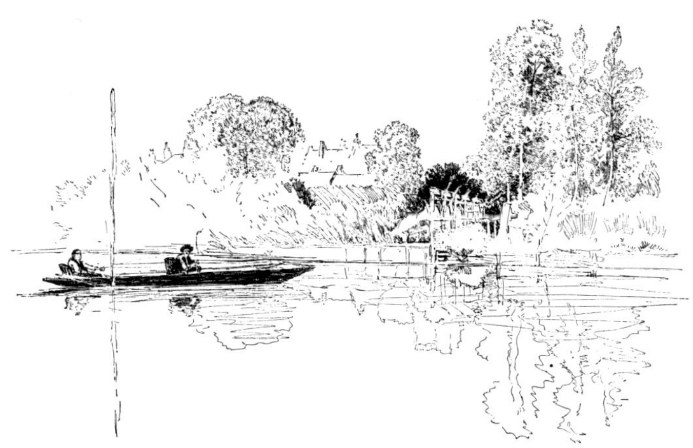

READING TO MARLOW

Reading, the county town and the largest in Berkshire, belies its ancient heritage, for here was once a castle and its abbey, founded by Henry I, ranked third of all in England. The town stands at the head of a ten mile stretch of river flowing down to Henley, which is deservedly among the most popular on the river.

At Sonning the old red-brick bridge, with its high centre arch, spans the water. The village is well-known but charming none the less. The lanes thread their way round sharp corners and between high walls, where plaster and black beams, and curious angles and gables combine in a most pleasing assembly.

Downstream, Wargrave soon comes into sight, facing the spacious flats of Shiplake meadows. This little village has a fine church with a Norman doorway. Thence it is but a mile or two to Henley, lying in a corner of Oxfordshire where three counties meet and as fine an example of an ancient country town as can be found. Straight as an arrow below the bridge stretches the balustraded Royal Regatta course, at the head of which the river divides around Temple Island before sweeping around the great Hambleden bend. In a quiet backwater beyond the lock on the Buckinghamshire bank nestles the picturesque, massive, weatherboarded Hambleden Mill, whilst further down the river on the Berkshire side is ancient Medmenham Abbey, redolent with the atmosphere of the Hellfire Club which met within its walls.

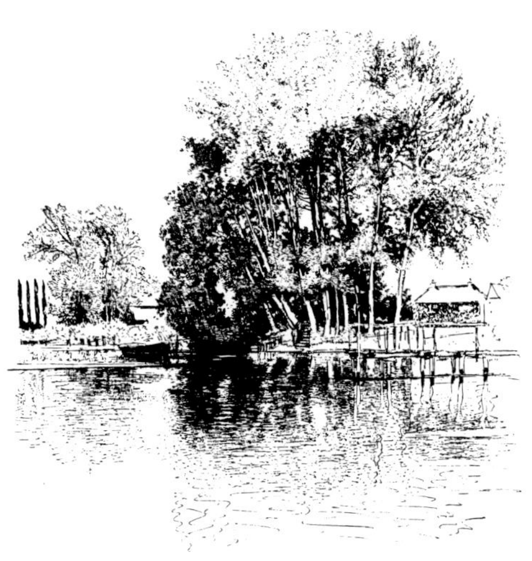

Upstream of Marlow the woods and private estates of Hurley, Temple and Bisham fill most of the low ground. In all the length of the Thames this is the one section where the "river country" is most noticeably narrowed down, for the Chilterns run close from the north, with Maidenhead Thicket to the south.

SONNING BRIDGE

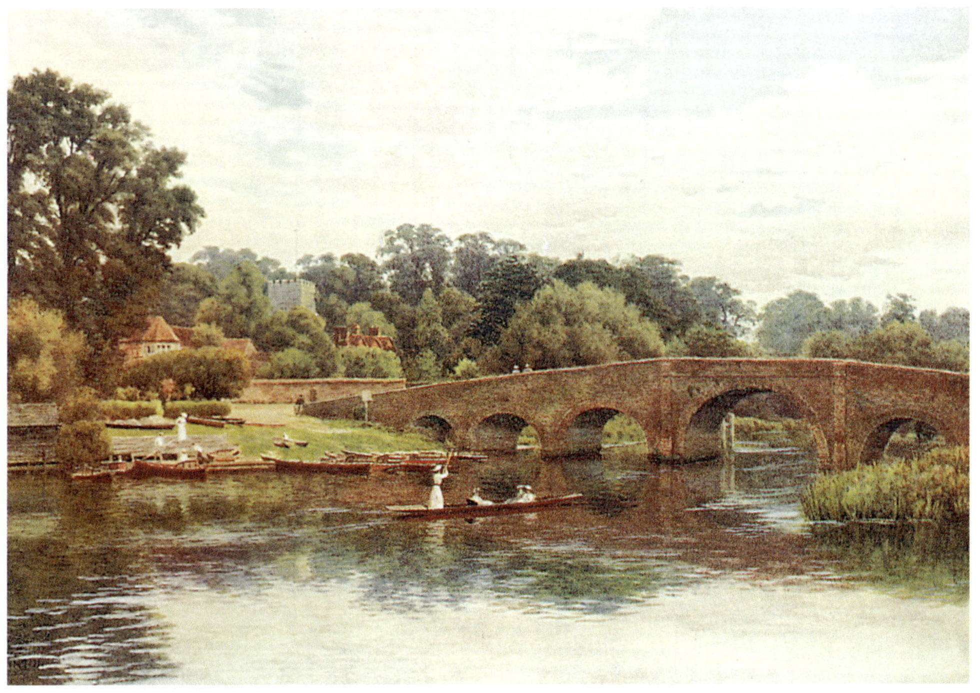

Trailing in the cool stream thy fingers wet,
As the slow punt swings round.

Matthew Arnold

SONNING VILLAGE

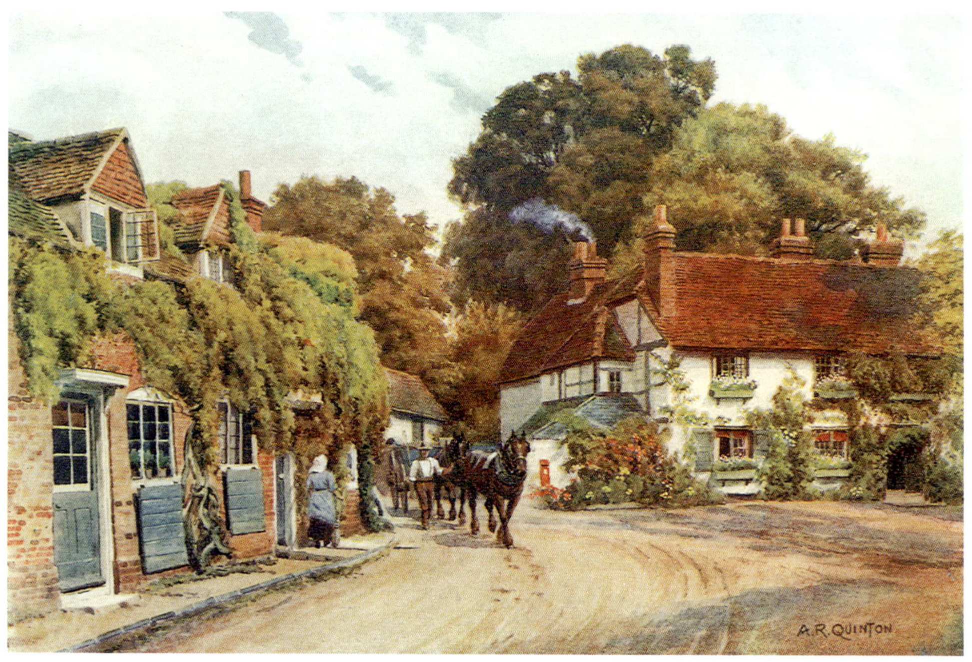

Soon will the musk carnations break and swell,
  Soon shall we have gold-dusted snapdragon,
Sweet-william with his homely cottage smell,
  And stocks in fragrant blow;

Matthew Arnold

THE GEORGE AND DRAGON INN, WARGRAVE

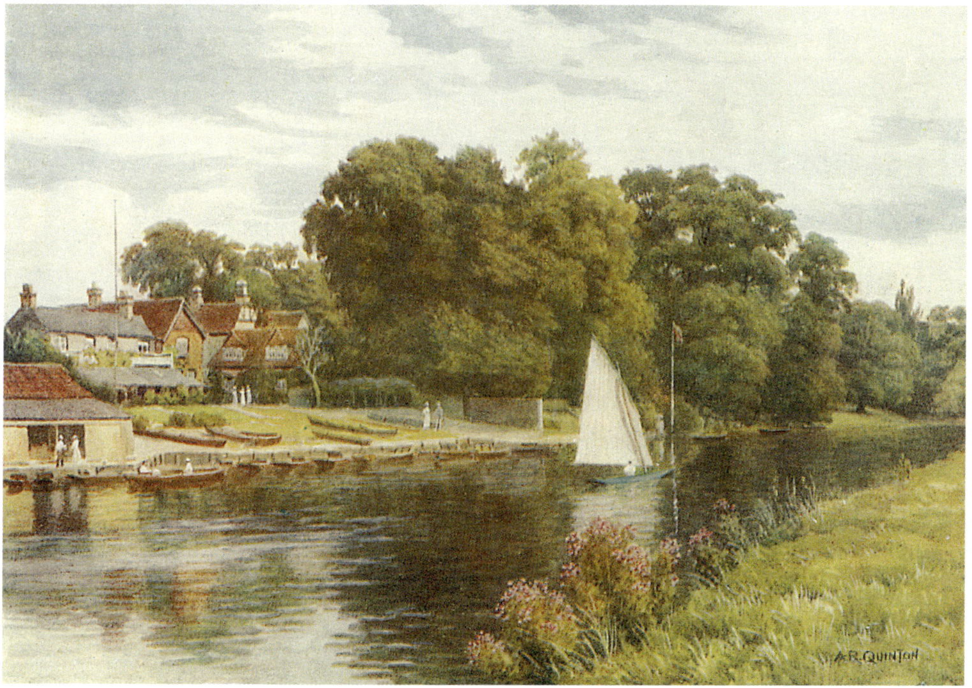

Whose turf, whose shade, whose flowers among
  Wanders the hoary Thames along its silver-winding way.

Thomas Gray

HAMBLEDEN WEIR AND MILL

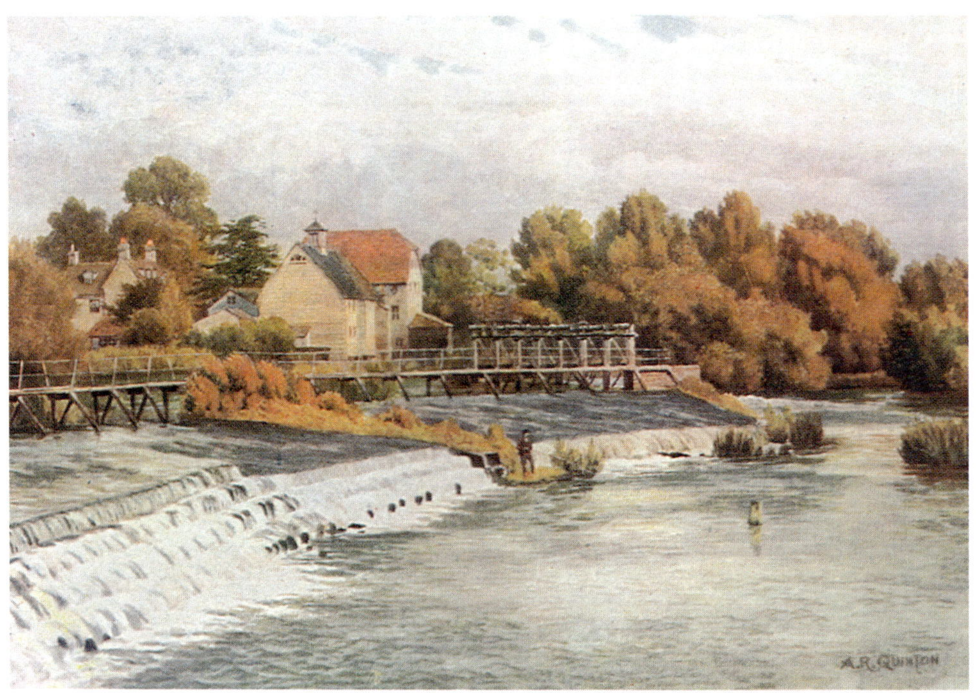

Where, with sound like many voices sweet
 Waterfalls leap among wild islands green.
Percy Bysshe Shelley

MARLOW FROM QUARRY WOODS

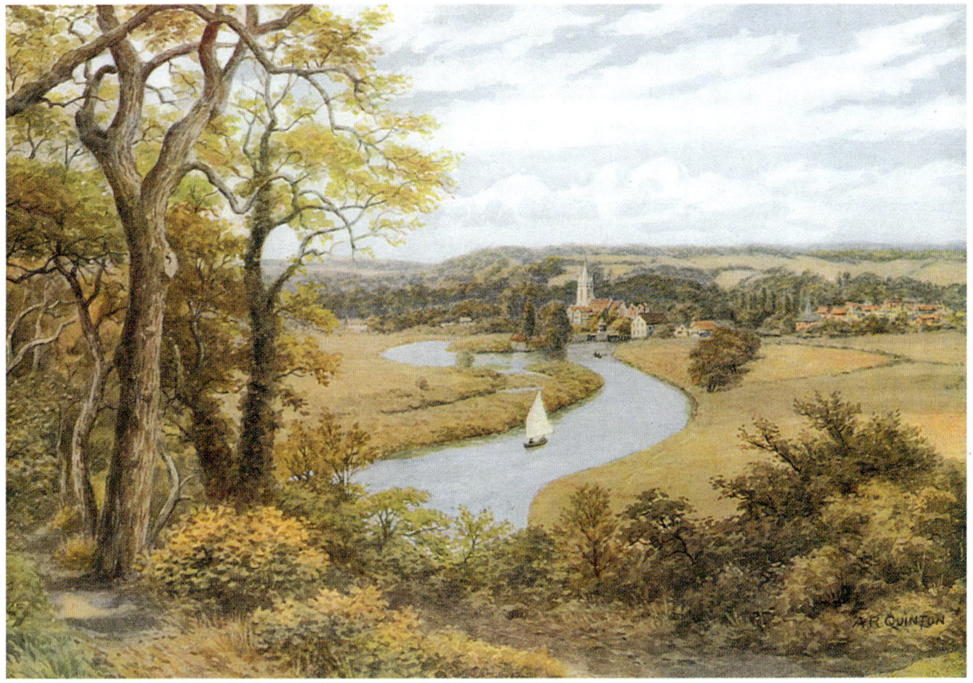

That beautiful valley, through which the Thames
rolls round the gentle hills of Berkshire.

Lord Macaulay

IN BOULTER'S LOCK

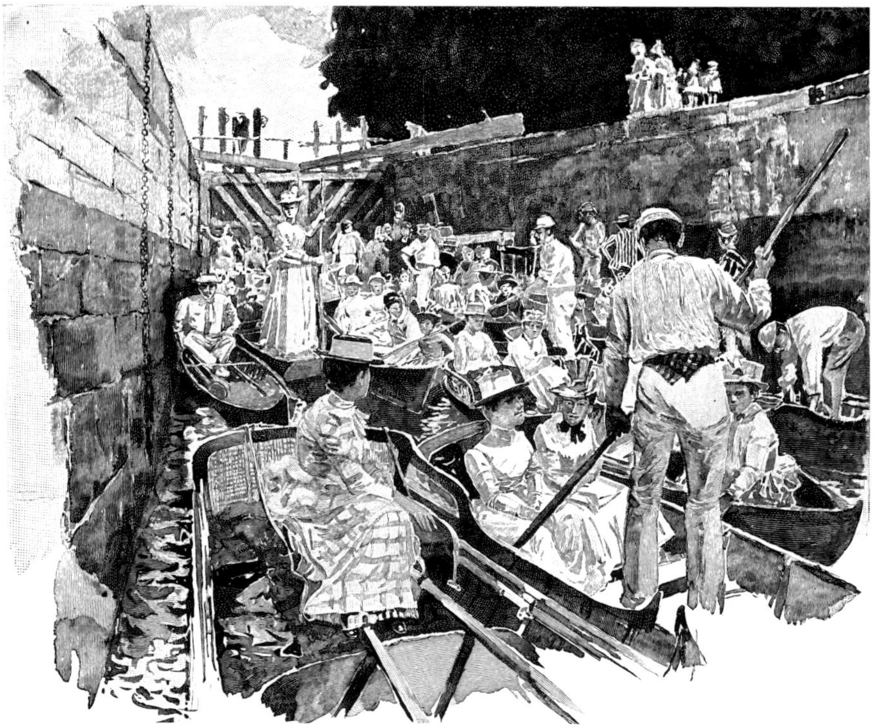

Presently the lock-keeper called out "Keep back!" and the lock gates slowly opened and out they came, pell-mell, pushing, paddling, poling, steaming, and there was great scrambling and bumping and brandishing of boathooks and scrunching of boats and scratching of paint.

Elizabeth R. Pennell

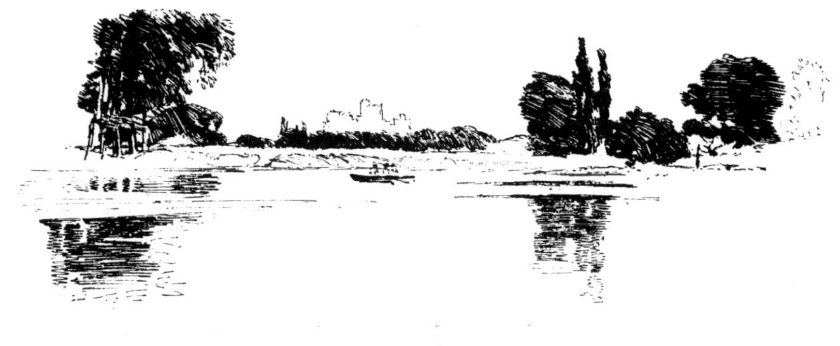

MARLOW TO WINDSOR

Marlow is a picturesque town, its wide main street running right on to the graceful suspension bridge. The high spire of the church rises close beside it, whilst the murmur of the water falling over the weir not far below is ever in one's ears. Below the weir, on the south side of the river, the curving sweep of famous Quarry Woods runs onwards to the green downs between Cookham and the scattered hamlet of Cookham Dean. Marlow's small neighbour, the village of Bisham, is a pleasant place with its line of cottages and its ancient abbey church on the very bank of the river. Originally a house of the Knights Templar, and later the Augustinians, its stout tower and oriel windows today make a fine picture.

Cookham Bridge, below which the river swings into its southerley course, is the prelude to the wide expanse of Cliveden

Reach with its attendant woods, thick with many varieties of trees; the various greens of oak, ash and chestnut and the deeper shades of fir and yew. High on the crest of the 140 feet high hill is the fine mansion of Cliveden, built for the Duke of Buckingham, a favourite of King Charles I. Below, the river flows on towards the civilisation of Boulter's Lock and Maidenhead, where the riverside promenade runs to the well-proportioned bridge. This was originally of wood and as far back as 1298 three oak trees from Windsor Forest were granted for its repair. Downstream, not very far above Monkey Island, is pretty little Bray, celebrated in verse by the ballad of the turncoat vicar, who in Tudor times changed his religious opinions to suit the vagaries of those turbulent dangerous times.

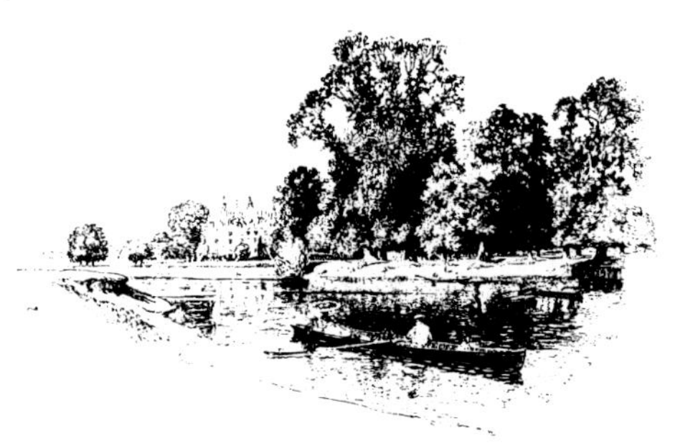

Monkey island is one of several small river islets just above Eton. It acquired its bizarre name from the frieze of grotesque monkeys painted on the ceiling in a quaint fishing lodge built on the island by the eccentric 2nd Duke of Marlborough.

From here the stream flows on towards Royal Windsor. The pinnacles of Eton College look out from one bank, whilst high on the other side is the mighty Round Tower of Windsor Castle. Standing on the bridge which links Windsor and Eton, the whole range of this splendid edifice can be held in sight, from the East Terrace to the Curfew Tower on the western end.

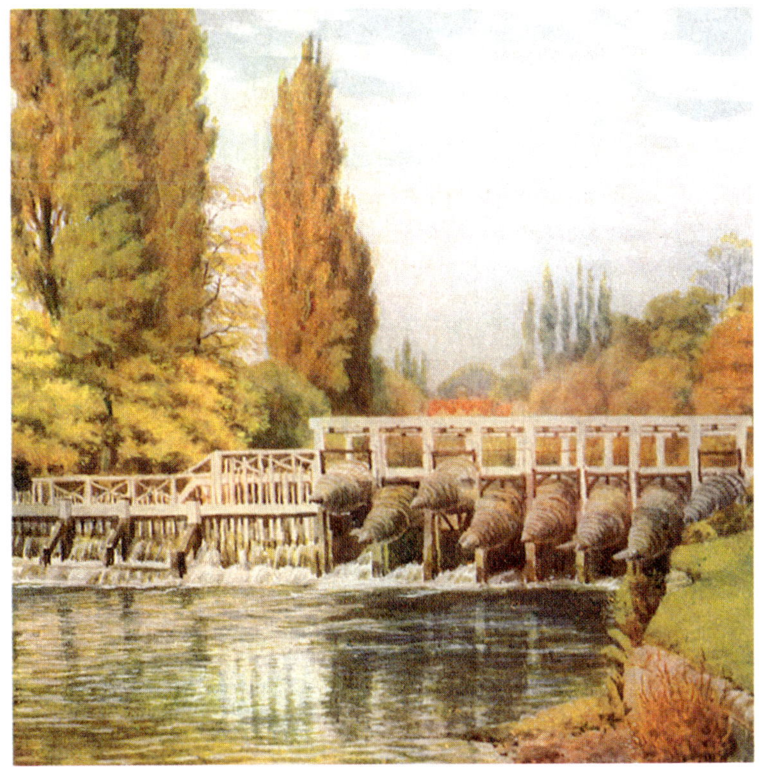

EEL-BUCKS AT HEDSOR
An appliance for catching eels migrating downstream

MY LADY FERRY, CLIVEDEN REACH

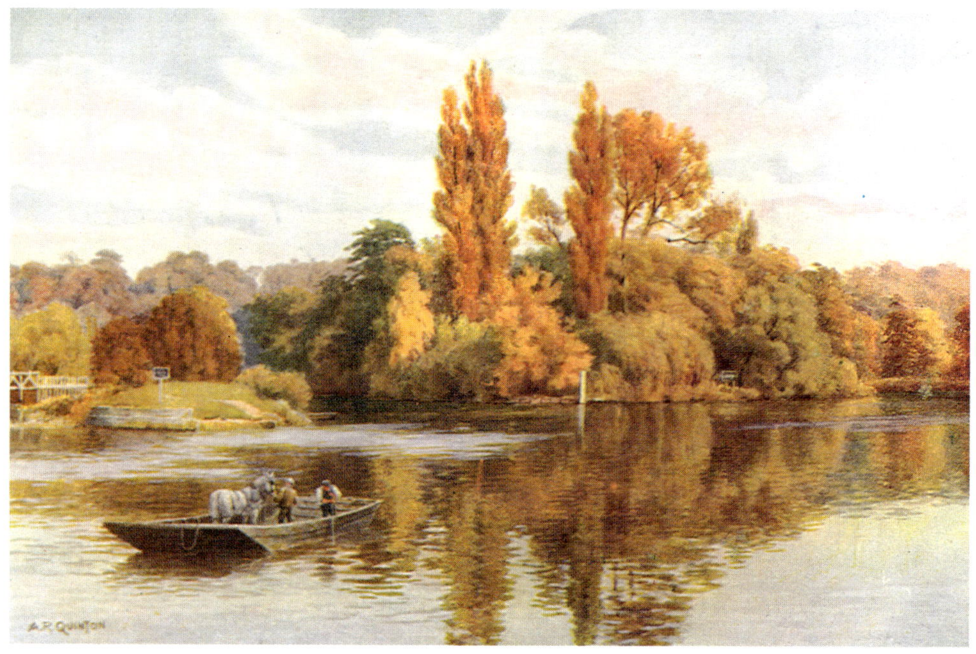

There are two things scarce matched in the Universe,
The sun in heaven and the Thames on earth.
Sir Walter Raleigh

BOULTER'S LOCK, MAIDENHEAD

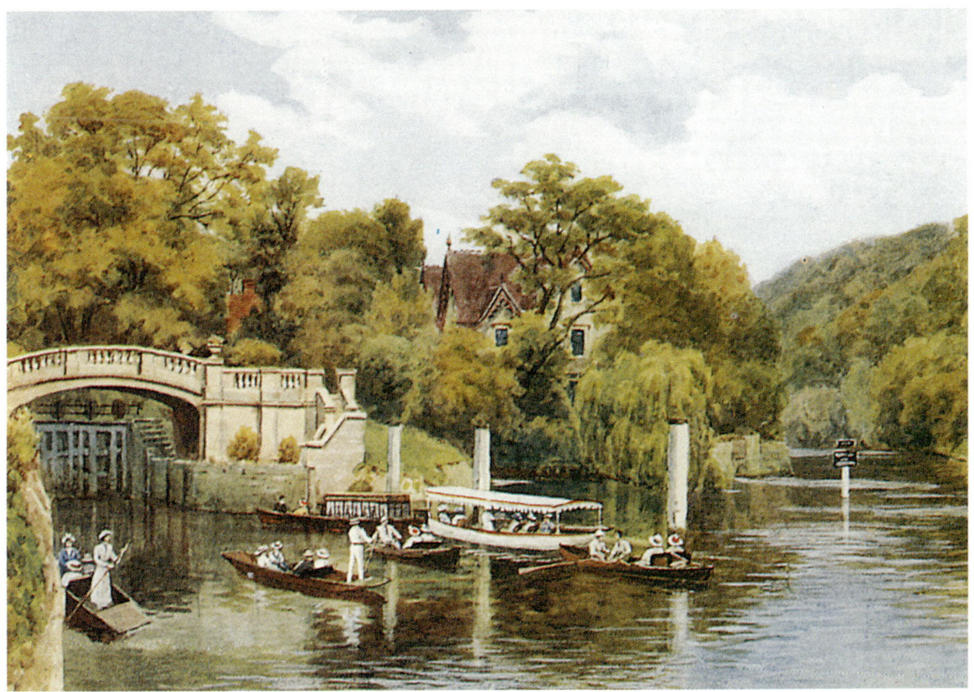

There is nothing – absolutely nothing – half so much worth doing as simply messing about in boats.

Kenneth Grahame

BRAY VILLAGE

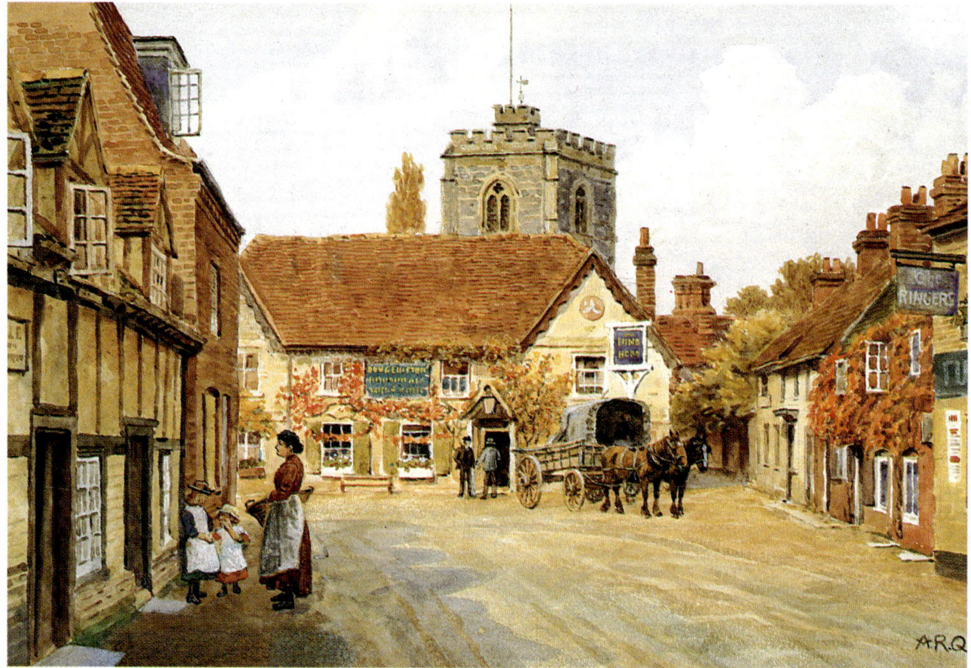

For this is law, I will maintain,
  Unto my dying day, Sir,
Whatever King in England reign
  I'll still be Vicar of Bray, Sir!

Anonymous

WINDSOR CASTLE

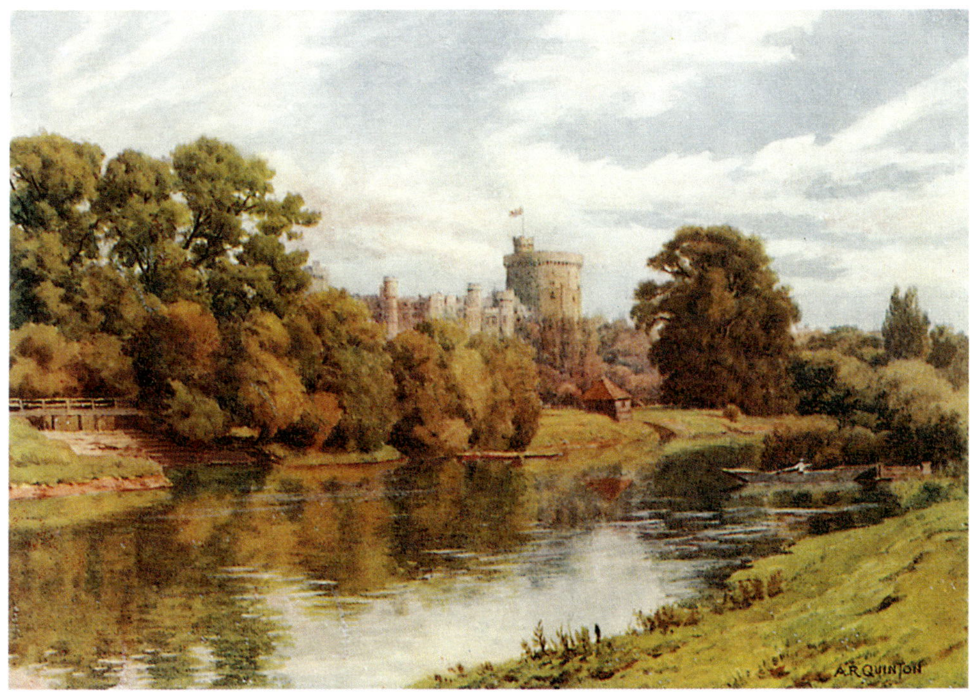

Every drop of the Thames is liquid history.
John Burns

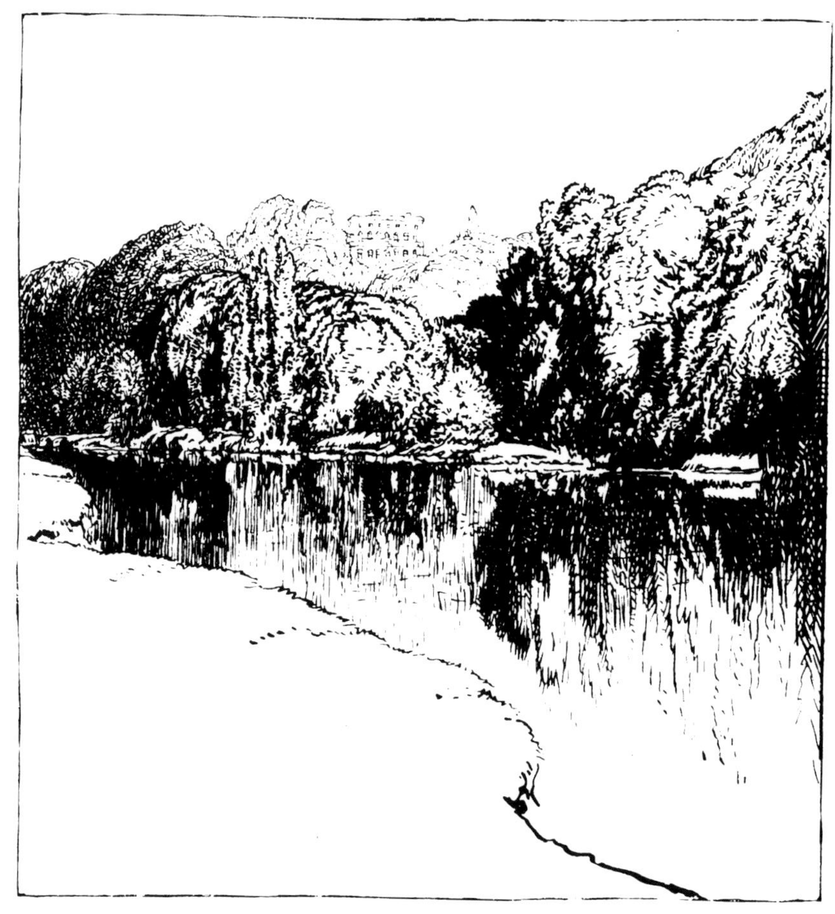

CLIVEDEN FROM THE THAMES

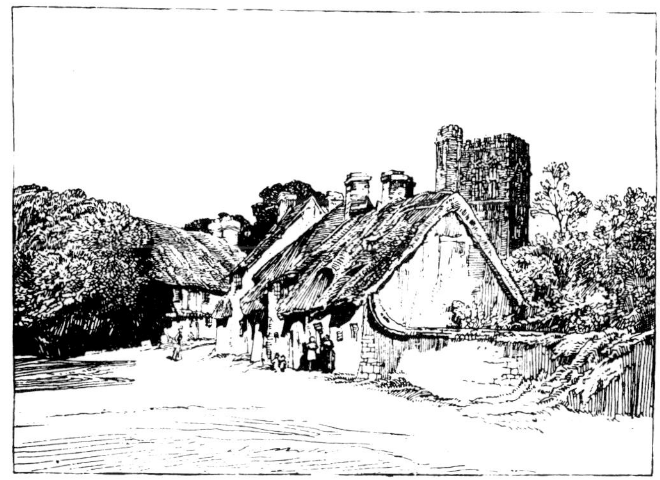

Long Crendon

IN CHILTERN COUNTRY

The county of Buckinghamshire has many attractions, not the least of which is its variety, for nothing could differ more than the wooded chalk slopes of the Chilterns, and the flat and rolling ground of the Vale of Aylesbury. Its towns and villages nestle in an aura of historical associations and scattered all about are fine examples of architecture, to be found by those who know where to look for them. These have their focus in the particularly fine medieval churches which lie hereabouts; magnificent Stewkley – pure Norman – pretty little Fingest with its gabled tower, the stout Norman tower at Haddenham and Long Crendon, with its attendant timbered Court House.

Few people have any idea of the number and variety of interesting associations, literary and otherwise, possessed by Buckinghamshire. At Stoke Poges, Thomas Gray wrote his "Elegy in a Country Churchyard", and some eight miles distant is Milton's Cottage at Chalfont St. Giles; of all the 17th century's poet many houses, this is the only one still standing and a delightful prospect it makes

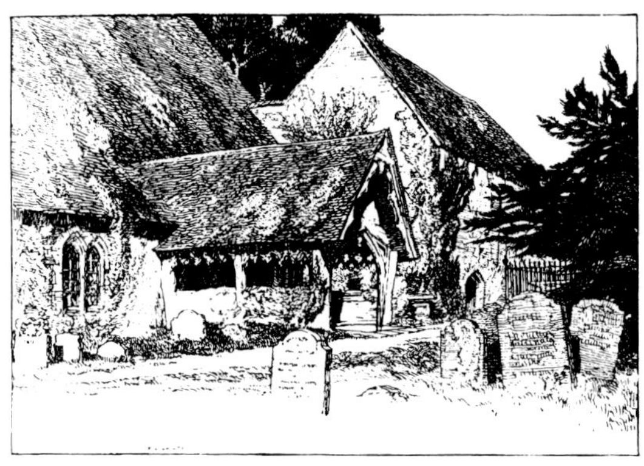

Stoke Poges Church

with its exterior chimney, gable-roof and wooden beams. It was here that Milton completed "Paradise Lost". Edmund Waller, poet and politician and, later Edmund Burke, lived at the old manor house at Beaconsfield and from here it is but a short step to Jordans, burial place of William Penn, the great Quaker and founder of Pennsylvania. From Beaconsfield the high road slopes north-westwards to High Wycombe; close by is Hughenden, home of Benjamin Disraeli, and up the beech-clad hills a few miles to the north is the home of John Hampden, who fought for Parliamentary liberty when Charles I sat on the throne.

AYLESBURY

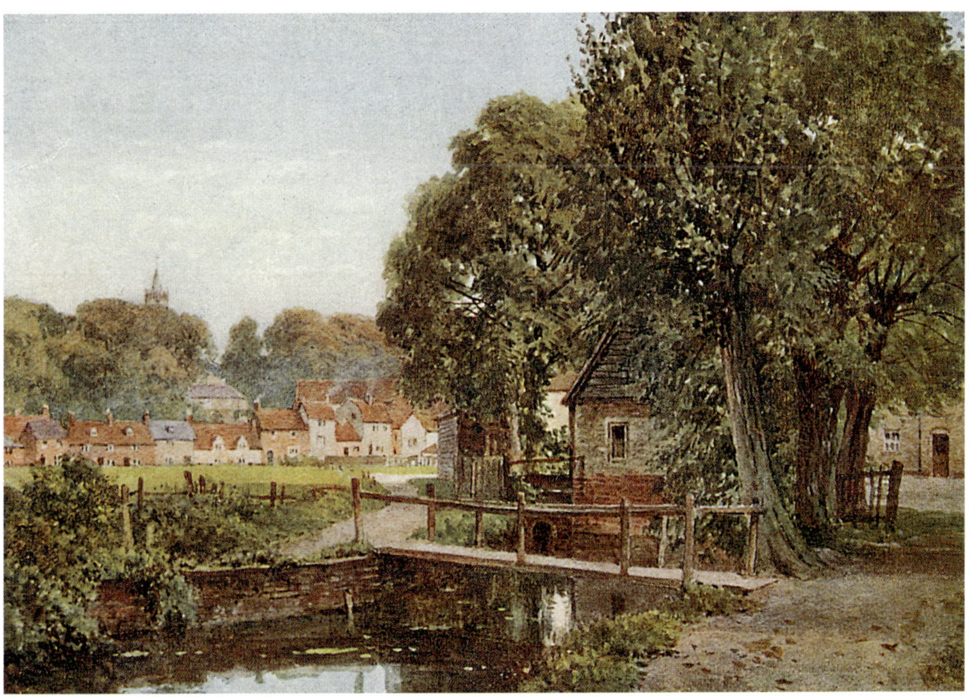

Aylesbury vale that walloweth in her wealth
  And, by her wholesome air continually in health,
Is lusty, firm and fat; and holds her youthful strength!

Michael Drayton

Extending across the county is the range of the Chilterns; the scenery shows the rolling, rounded outlines always associated with the chalk. The contrast of the glory in the fields and the darkness of the woods that crown them is very fine – amidst the hills are lush, green bottoms and an abundance of rushing streams. Beyond lies the level ground in the neighbourhood of Aylesbury.

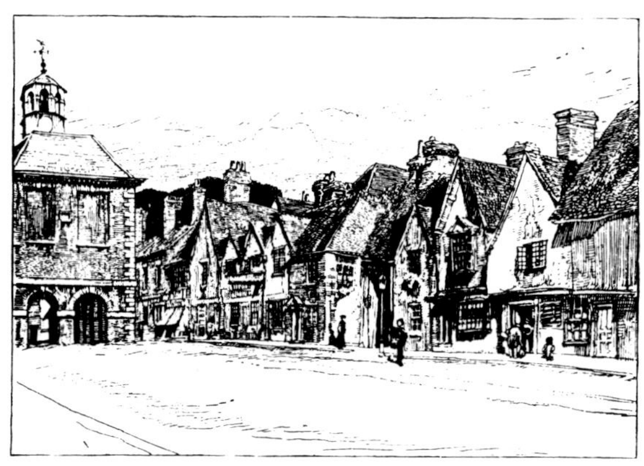

Amersham

Aylesbury itself is a pleasant town, with a fine bronze statue of John Hampden and a splendid church. The surrounding vale is green and fertile – to the south the blue rampart of the Chilterns rears across the skyline, whilst northwards the ground is prolonged in great rolling ridges. On the summits lie Upper Winchendon and Brill, surveying the countryside from its 600 feet vantage point whilst in the valley bottoms are Lower Winchendon and Cuddington, rich in colour-washed homesteads and the riotous colour of cottage gardens.

THE WINDMILL, BRILL

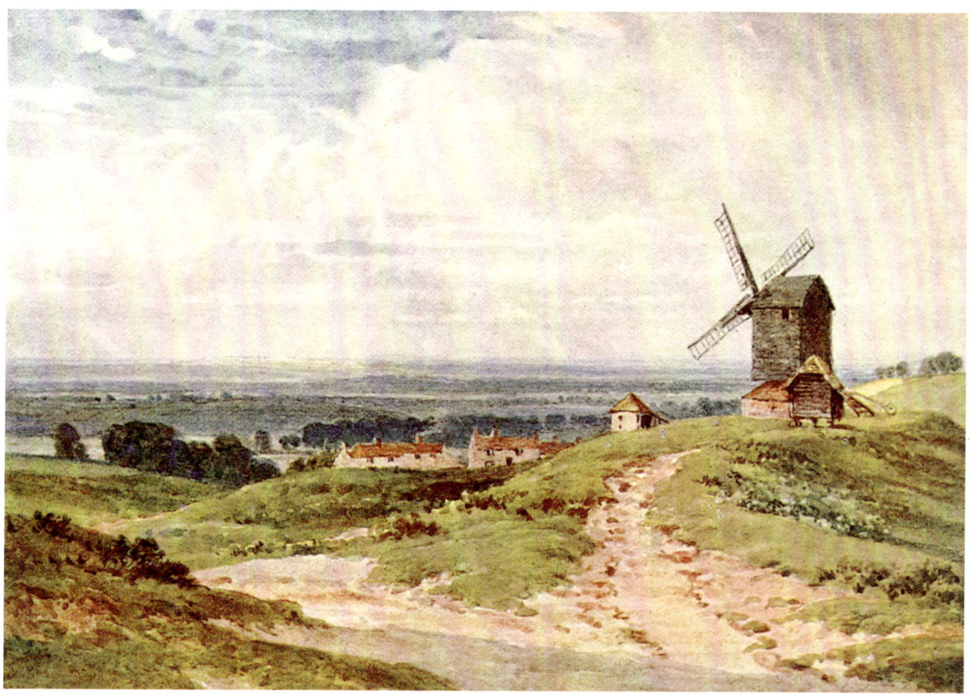

Here, in full light the russet plains extend;
 There, wrapt in clouds the bluish hills ascend.

Alexander Pope

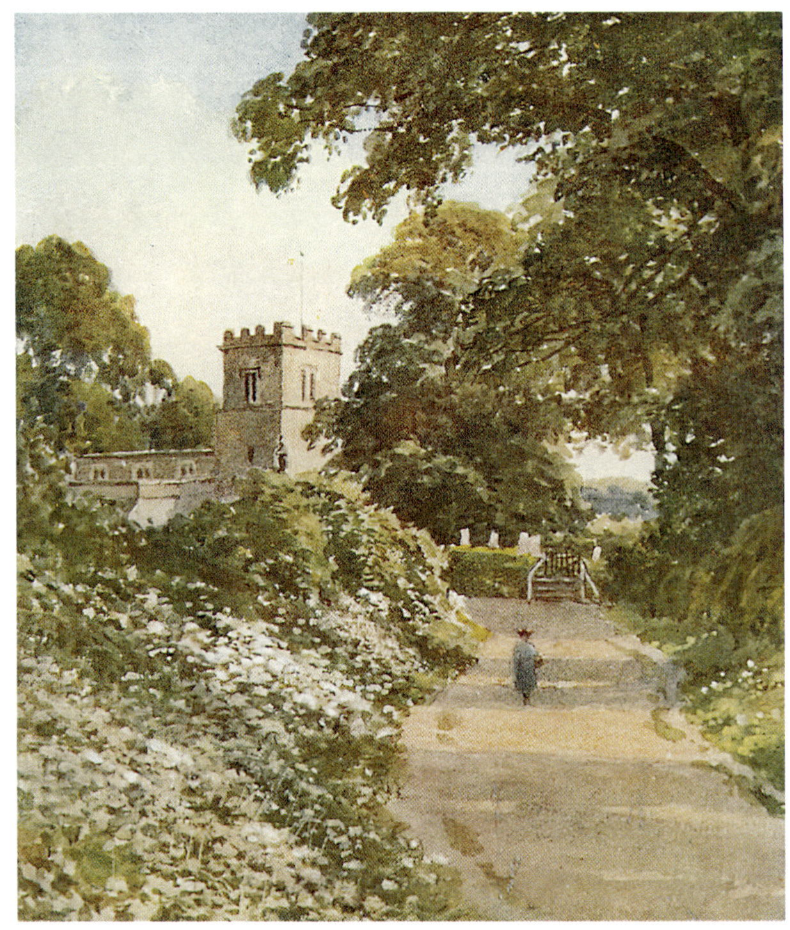

GREAT MISSENDEN

PRINCES RISBOROUGH

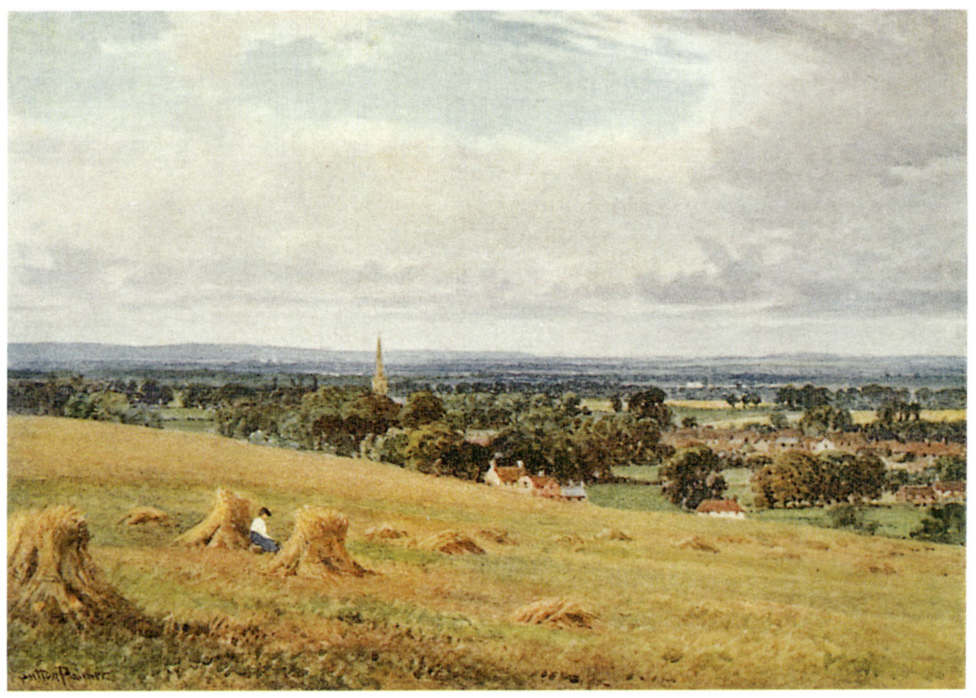

While far beyond, and overthwart the stream,
  That, as with molten glass, inlays the vale,
The sloping land recedes into the clouds.

William Cowper

CHALFONT ST. GILES

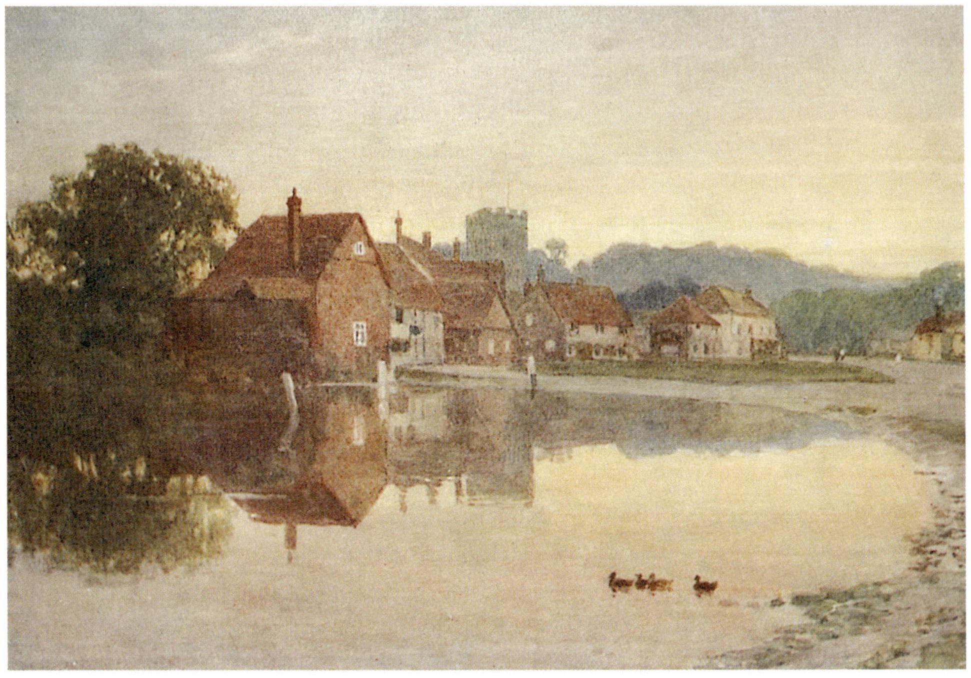

I know each lane and every alley green
  Dingle or bushy dell of this wild wood,
And every bosky bourne from side to side;
  My daily walks and ancient neighbourhood.

John Milton

BURNHAM BEECHES

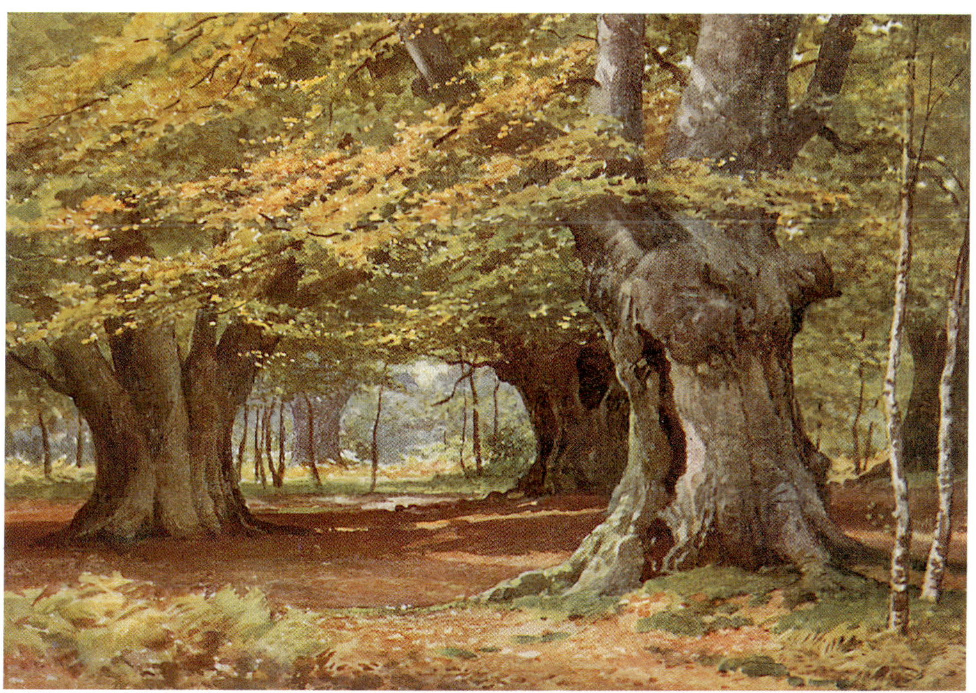

Where'er the oak's thick branches stretch
  A broader, browner shade;
Where'er the rude and moss-grown beech
  O'ercanopies the glade.

Thomas Gray

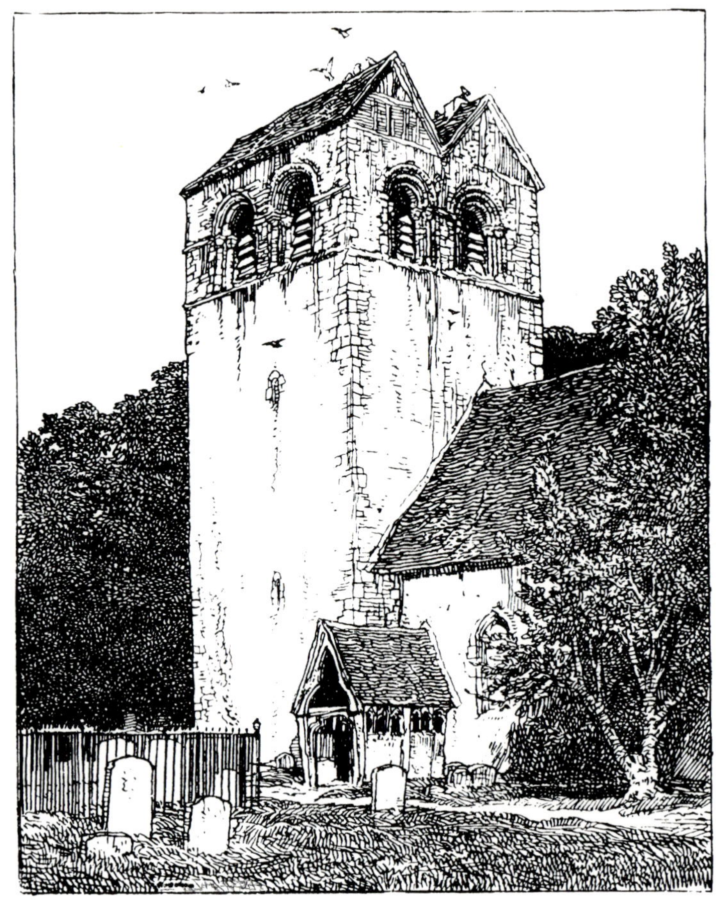

FINGEST CHURCH